A Shiksa's Guide to Jewish Marriage:
The to-dos before "I do"!

Helpful Tips for Planning a Traditional Jewish Wedding

MARCELLE SIRKUS

Dedicated to my son, Jake.

— M.S.

INTRODUCTION

You're engaged?! Mazel tov!

(That means "Congratulations")

[SHIK-zah = Jewish term for a non-Jewish woman]

So you're getting married! How exciting! And to a nice Jewish boy?! Mazel tov! But what if you're *not* a Jewish girl?

By now, you may already be familiar with the term *shiksa*. The word *shiksa* is of Yiddish origin, used to describe a non-Jewish woman.

Among Orthodox Jews, the term *shiksa* may even be used to describe a *Jewish* woman, but one who does not fully conform to Orthodox religious rules and edicts.

When it comes to planning a Jewish wedding, there are many unique rules and traditions which you may want to explore. You may choose to include them as you prepare to join your beloved at the ceremonial altar (in Judaism we call that the *bimah*, pronounced BEE-mah), or you might want to tweak the rules to suit you and partner as you see fit. Or perhaps you may decide to opt out of them altogether.

I'm what you might call a *shiksa-Jew*. Am I Jewish? Yes, I am! Did I follow all the Jewish wedding traditions when I married my Jewish husband? No, I did not. But I did include many of the traditions, which helped to make our special day wonderful and memorable.

On the following pages, we'll explore some of these traditions together. I'll share a few personal experiences and tips along the way!

Tip #1

Shidduch happens.

[SHID-uk = a system of Jewish matchmaking]

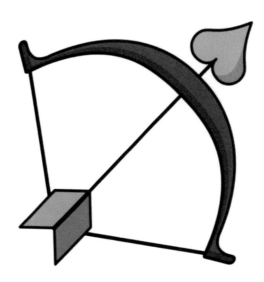

Matchingmaking has been a Jewish tradition for ages. There is hardly an unmarried Jewish adult on planet Earth who has not been asked at least once (or maybe a *hundred* times) by a parent, grandparent, or senior family member, "Are you still *single*?! I've got someone nice for you to meet!"

In the Jewish community matchmaking is serious business. Finding suitable suitors for Semitic singles is a profession unto itself. These matchmakers are called *shadchans* (pronounced SHAHD-kehns) — they perform the service of working to hook up singles within the Jewish community thereby making a *shidduch.*

So, while *shidduch* happens, and matchmaking is actively practiced in many cultures, your beloved doesn't need this service because he's already found *you*! And *you* are his *bashert.* (bah-SHAYRT = Yiddish word for "soul mate.")

Tip #2
Save the date!
[CAL-en-duh = choose wisely, not just *any* date will do]

The excitement is building! You're engaged and ready to kick off the wedding planning. That all starts with setting the wedding date.

Depending on how religiously observant you or your partner is, this can be a bit tricky. There are guidelines for when a Jewish wedding ceremony may be performed — and strict guidelines for when it may *not* be performed.

So if you plan on making it a Jewish-affair, it will be important to clear the date with an expert in these matters. If you already have a rabbi to perform the traditional ceremony, the rabbi will be able to advise you accordingly.

Generally, the wedding can take place any day of the week, but may not occur during the Jewish Sabbath beginning sundown on Friday evening through sundown on Saturday, or during major Jewish holidays when those observing are prohibited from travel and work.

Tip #3
Yiddish–English Cheat Sheet
[YID-ish = language spoken by Jewish people in Eastern Europe,
originally based on a German dialect]

Yiddish is sometimes confused with Hebrew. But they are not one and the same. Hebrew is the ancient language of the Israelites and their ancestors, and is the official language of the State of Israel. Yiddish is the unofficial language of the Eastern European Jewish people dating back to the early 1200s. Yiddish is a mix of German dialects along with bits and pieces of Russian, Polish, and other Slavic languages.

When I was a little kid, my grandmother would use Yiddish words when she didn't want me to understand what she was saying. But it didn't take me too long to figure out some of it. For example, "Kish mir en tuches" is easily decoded into the English translation, "Kiss my ass"!

Over the course of your relationship with your Jewish significant other, you might find yourself at social gatherings in which Yiddish words may be spoken.

Even without the following cheat sheet, you may be able to get the gist of it.
That said, I'm here to help. So let's dive in . . . .

OY = Geez.

OY VEY = OMG.

OY GAVALT = Holy crap!

GOY = A non-Jewish man.

SHIKSA = A non-Jewish woman.

BUBBE (BUB-bee) = Grandmother.

ZAYDE (ZAY-duh) = Grandfather.

MESHUGENER = Silly or crazy person.

MISHEGAS = Craziness, chaos.

NOSH = To eat; or, a snack.

BUPKIS = A very small amount or near nothing at all (literally means "goat droppings").

GELT = Money.

FEH = Not good; an expression of dislike or disapproval.

MEH = Not bad or good; generally indifferent.

GAY KOCKEN = Idiom that means "Get outta here with your silliness. Beat it. I'm not interested." Literally means, "Go take a shit."

GAY KOCKEN OFFEN YOM = Idiom, similar to *gay kocken*. Means "Go take a shit in the ocean." (You may be asking, "Why is *this* a saying?" No one knows for sure.)

KISH MIR EN TUCHES = Kiss my ass.

KISHKA = Guts or stomach; a type of sausage or stuffed intestine.

KOSHER = In accordance with Jewish law; typically refers to food, food-prep, or the kitchen.

SCHMOOZE = Chat it up with others at an informal gathering.

KIBBITZ = To wisecrack, joke around and hang out with friends. Example: "On Sunday my friends and I are meeting at the Canter's Deli Kibbitz Room to schmooze and kibbitz."

SCHMALTZ = Literally means "chicken fat"; also used to describe an overly sentimental story as "schmaltzy."

YENTA = A gossiper or busybody.

NU = What's up?! Also means "Well?" or "So?"

DRECK = Dirt or trash, and sometimes "shit."

ZELBE DRECK = Same shit (different day); acceptable answer to the question "Nu?"

TCHATCHKE (CHACH-kuh) = Knick knack, or little gift.

TUCHES = Rear end, backside, buttocks.

SCHMATTE (SHMAH-tuh) = Raggedy clothes or tattered garment.

SCHMUCK = A man who is a jerk (also literal term for "penis").
This reminds me of a joke . . . well, it's really not in the best taste, so I'll take a pass on this for the moment.

SCHLEP = To carry or lug; also means an arduous trek or journey.
Example: "You're gonna shlep all the way to Staten Island just for a slice of pizza?!"

PUTZ = A another term for a man who is a jerk (also literal term for "penis").

KVEL = A feeling of overwhelming pride.

BISSEL = A little bit. Example: "I'll have a bissel of potato salad."

SHTICKLE = A piece. Example: "Just one shtickle of cake, please! I have to fit into a wedding dress soon."

SHTICK = Silly humorous action or gimmick; comic routine; bit.

CHUTZPAH (KHOOTS-puh) = Bold; shamelessness or audacity.

MISHPOCHEH (mish-POOK-uh) = Your family or your peeps, gathered together.
Example: "On Super Bowl Sunday we had the whole mishpocheh over to watch the game."

BALABOSTE (BAHL-uh-buhst) = A thoughtful and generous host. (If you're hosting the whole mishpocheh at your home on Super Bowl Sunday, you're a balaboste!)

SHVITZ = A steam bath or sauna; to sweat.

SPIEL = A long story. This word always makes me think of Steven Spielberg, who is a wonderful storyteller! And since the word *berg* can mean a town or place, it makes me wonder: Could the name *Spielberg* literally mean "town of great story tellers"?

MENSCH = An honorable person; a decent and thoughtful man.

MAZEL TOV = Means good fortune or "Congratulations"; occasionally used sarcastically.
Example: "Wow, you put your own dishes in the sink after you were done eating? Mazel tov!"

Tip #4
Ring-a-ding-ding. *This* ring's got no bling!
[WEH-ding ring = symbol of the marriage]

Wedding rings are an important part of the traditional Jewish wedding — just as they are in most wedding ceremonies. However, you may notice that the particular wedding rings pictured above are completely absent of jewels, crafty designs, or adornments of any kind.

This is intentional.

The bride's ring, intended to be a gesture of commitment by the groom, must not be "broken" in any way. The solidity of the Jewish wedding band solidifies the ring's value, as well as the couple's commitment to marriage, symbolizing the union to be whole and everlasting. The wedding band itself must be a plain solid metal, without any cuts or etching. So don't go chipping away at the ring's surface to glue in any pesky jewels, diamonds, emeralds and the like.

If you want to keep this tradition for the ceremony, but prefer a ring with bling, there's a simple solution: two sets of rings! A traditional metal-only unadorned ring may be exchanged during the wedding ceremony — and any other rings you and your partner choose may be worn afterwards.

Tip #5
Yarmulkes. Not just for Hanukkah!
[YAH-muh-kuh = traditional Jewish skullcap, also known as a *kippah*]

During a Jewish wedding ceremony, the male guests typically don a skullcap (also called "yarmulke" or "kippah"). In fact, whether or not the attendees are Jewish, all male guests generally will wear yarmulkes at the event out of respect for the occasion.

Religiously observant Jewish women may cover their hair, or wear a lace head covering. In some Jewish communities, the women wear the traditional yarmulkes, too.

The hosts of the wedding are expected to provide the skullcaps so that their guests do not have to bring their own. There are multitudinous styles, fabrics, sizes, and trims available for order on the Internet — and they often include custom messaging on the inner lining, where you may inscribe your name and that of your beloved, along with the date of the wedding.

It makes a great keepsake, so order lots of extras!

Bonus Tip: Order your yarmulkes well ahead of your wedding date. Last year, I ordered five dozen yarmulkes more than 12 weeks before my son's bar mitzvah from a local shop to be sure to have them on time. But they arrived with a typo on the inscription! They misspelled my son's name! The shopkeeper resubmitted the entire order back to the supplier. When the second batch arrived, they came in with the wrong color trim. I finally got my order — just two days before the affair! What a headache it was!

Tip #6
Ketubah time! Sign on the dotted line!
[kuh-TOO-bah = traditional Jewish marriage contract]

As the wedding date gets closer, you may be reminded to start shopping for your ketubah, or wedding contract. Note: This is not a prenup in the sense that it does not attempt to restrict assets in the event of a break-up, but a declaration which specifically calls out the husband's obligations to his wife, and documents the provisions for her protection in the event of divorce or of the husband's demise.

One of the earliest ketubahs still in existence was found in Egypt, written on papyrus.

Today, ketubahs may be purchased from most Judaica shops. And on the Internet, too. There are literally thousands of websites that sell ketubahs in a variety of shapes, sizes, colors, and styles, from traditional to modern — and everything in between.

Bonus Tip: Each member of wedding party may provide a witness to sign the ketubah before the wedding ceremony begins. Traditionally, the signatures are to be affixed in Hebrew. Your witnesses should be advised well in advance to prepare to write in Hebrew, if that is desired.

Tip #7

Eat, drink, and be married!

[KO-shur = kosher; food prepared in accordance with Jewish dietary law]

The decision whether or not to host kosher meals at your wedding will greatly determine what's on the menu, and not just as it pertains to the food. Serving strictly kosher fare impacts everything from the cocktails, wine, and mixers, to the meals, treats, coffees, and cakes. And the wedding cake, too!

One of the most widely known features of the kosher menu is that dairy products may not be served at the same time as meat. So if you are serving kosher and including meat meals, know that there must be non-dairy accompaniments served. Coffee must have non-dairy creamers. Butter should be replaced with non-dairy substitutes. The whipped cream and icing on your wedding cake will need to be non-dairy as well.

Often, the decision whether or not to serve kosher, and strictly adhering to the rules thereof, is primarily determined by the venue that is hosting the affair. If you are planning to wed at a conservative Jewish temple, then it is likely that the venue will require that you stick to the kosher-food rules.

If the chosen venue is a reform temple (where they may have less strict rules) or a private venue like a hotel or other locale, then you have the option to do kosher, or not to do, or to offer both options — whatever you like!

Tip #8
The hoopla is at the chuppah!
[HOO-pah, or hoo-PAH = a canopy under which a wedding ceremony is performed]

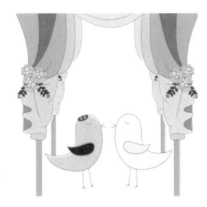

Whether indoors or out-of-doors, you'll likely *not* see a Jewish wedding ceremony take place without the traditional chuppah — a canopy typically constructed of four posts covered above with cloth or a tallit (TAHL-eat = traditional Jewish prayer shawl), and flowers. The chuppah is a symbol of home with the intentional absence of walls, to symbolize openness and hospitality.

The groom will enter the chuppah first, to represent that he has provided this home for his bride. When the bride enters the chuppah, her waiting groom is declaring publicly that he has prepared this home for her, offering himself to ensure her care and well-being.

The chuppah itself may rest on the floor, or you may ask family members to hold and support the posts throughout the ceremony.

Bonus Tip: If there's a chance that the rabbi at your ceremony will talk even half as long as the rabbi at *my* ceremony (which felt like *forever*) I suggest you place the chuppah firmly on the ground to minimize distractions, and save your guests a lengthy upper-arm workout.

Tip #9
Would you like some tea with your *mikvah*?
[MIK-vuh = a Jewish ritual bath]

During the planning of our wedding, my future husband asked me if I had remembered to make arrangements for a pre-wedding *mikvah*. "Say *what* now?" I asked.

"Mikvah," he repeated, "You know. . . it's the spa thing."

I had never heard the word *mikvah* before. But I thought, a special bridal spa day sounds pretty good. I'm in! But just to be sure, I decided I'd better do a little bit of research first, just to be sure of what I was getting into.

A mikvah is a traditional ritual pre-wedding bath, typically at a traditional mikvah facility, for a prayer-filled purifying cleanse. It's kind of like a baptism, except naked. And not alone!

The mikvah comes complete with an attendant (female) who will check you for stray hairs or other "debris" before you enter the purified water, while her main function is to make sure that the top of your head and all your hair completely enters the water when you are dunked.

As observed by very religious Jews, it is required by Jewish law to visit the mikvah once a month — seven days after menstruation. And since it is also protocol to abstain from sex while the woman is on her period, that adds up to about two weeks out of each month that the married couple will be expected to abstain from intimacy altogether.

I've heard that the mikvah is a lovely experience, though I wouldn't happen to know first-hand. I graciously declined. It didn't sound like my cup of tea.

If you *do* decide to participate in this pre-wedding ritual, be sure to request a checklist from the facility on how to prepare. Everything from when to get a haircut to shaving, waxing, make-up removal, fingernail prep, ear cleaning and proper pre-soak nose blowing are to be performed at specific intervals prior to the mikvah.

Bon voyage!

Tip #10

Checkin' at the bedeken!

[buh-DECK-in = ceremonial visit by the bridegroom to "check out" his bride

before the wedding ceremony]

The bedeken is a traditional ceremony that takes place just before the wedding nuptials. The groom, typically accompanied by his father (or father-in-law, or whomever will be escorting the groom down the aisle) is escorted to a room where the bride awaits the visit.

The groom greets his bride and ceremoniously places the veil over the bride's face. Doing this task assures the groom that he has seen the bride that he is about to declare his commitment to, and thus ensures that when the marriage is pronounced official and the veil is lifted, there won't be any surprises — the groom can be certain that the bride he's chosen will be the same gal at the altar.

There are many stories that proclaim to be the origin of this tradition. My personal favorite is the ol' "bait and switch." According to the biblical story of Jacob, he was expecting to marry the lovely and fair Rachel. However, he was sorely disappointed at the end of his own wedding ceremony when he lifted the bridal veil to find that he had in fact married "the lesser babka" (as Elaine Benes might describe it) — Rachel's *sister* Leah.

And so, we have the bedeken — for a quick sneak-peek, just to be sure!

Tip #11
Let's take a vote for *hakafot*!
[hah-kah-FOHT = Hebrew word that means "circling"]

A familiar tradition at a Jewish wedding ceremony is the "Seven Circles," referred to using the Hebrew word *hakafot*. At the beginning of the wedding, the bride walks around the groom, circling him seven times around. There are many interpretations of the significance of the number seven, and of the bride performing this rite.

The bride's circles may symbolize the breaking down of any walls between them, signifying their union as a couple. This is based on the story of Joshua circling the walls of Jericho; after seven times around, the walls came tumbling down. Alternatively, the bride circling the groom may be seen as a gesture to build up a wall of protection for the groom, and of the couple.

The number seven appears as the number of days of creation; the wedding ceremony is the start of the creation of a new household. The phrase "when a man takes a wife" occurs in the Bible seven times. The number seven also corresponds to the Seven Blessings, often chanted or sung during the ceremony.

Bonus Tip: Many modern couples choose to modify this tradition by circling each other, demonstrating equality within their relationship.

Tip #12
Sheva me timbers and set sail for the seven blessings!
[SHEH-vuh BREK-oat = the seven wedding blessings]

Toward the latter part of your wedding ceremony, the rabbi or officiant may begin the reciting of the *Sheva Brachot*, the Seven Blessings. They may be read or chanted, or sung by a cantor — an individual who is ordained and typically professionally musically trained to chant the worship services in the temple (also called a *synagogue*).

The blessings, said over a cup of wine, give thanks for the creation of the universe, the creation of humanity, and the joining of people in unity and love, along with a blessing for the joy of marriage, and more.

In some modern Jewish ceremonies, the couple may choose to interpret and even adapt their own blessings to be read aloud by various members of the wedding party, family members, and guests.

The blessings are typically recited in Hebrew. They may be translated into English as well.

Tip #13
Meet the tallit!
[tahl-EAT= traditional Jewish prayer shawl]

The *tallit*, traditional Jewish prayer shawl, is worn by the groom during the wedding ceremony. At 13 years of age, young men receive their own tallit during bar mitzvah (or at their bat mitzvah, for young women) — the religious ceremony in which they recite Jewish prayers and are welcomed into the Jewish community, to worship and to observe religious precepts.

Alternatively, a bride may give her groom a tallit prior to the ceremony as a wedding gift.

The chuppah at the wedding ceremony may also be draped with a tallit — as a covering atop the canopy.

During the final blessing of the marriage ceremony, the bride and groom may be wrapped in the tallit, across both their shoulders, to symbolize their unity and surrounding them with love.

Tip #14
Kiddush rhymes with Yiddish.
[KI-dish = Jewish prayer and blessing over wine]

The Kiddush is the prayer and blessing over wine to give thanks for the creation of the fruit of the vine. The blessing of the wine kicks off the betrothal ceremony. Kosher wine should be selected, sealed, and placed in the chuppah, along with two cups.

Traditionally, the kiddush cups are made from gold or silver, but may also be made from fine china, pewter, or pottery.

While red wine is most typically presented, white wine works, too. Which is good to know, if you're nervous about the prospect of accidently spilling red wine on your wedding togs!

Bonus Tips:
- If you and your partner don't drink wine, grape juice (red or white) is an acceptable substitute.
- No need to chug it all down. A ceremonial sip will do!

Tip #15
In case of celebration, break glass!
[BRAYK-glass = tradition of stepping on a glass at the end of the marriage ceremony]

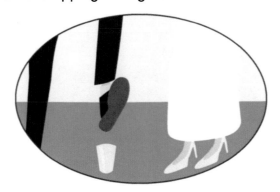

If you've ever attended a Jewish wedding or seen one on TV, you're likely familiar with this time-honored tradition: At the end of the Jewish marriage ceremony, a drinking glass wrapped in a cloth is placed at the foot of the groom. The groom fervently smashes the glass with his right foot, signalling the end of the ceremony. The happy newlyweds kiss and the crowd cheers, "Mazel tov!"

The exact origin of this tradition is not known, though many have speculated. Some believe that it is reminder to mourn the historic destruction of the Temple in Jerusalem, never to be forgotten even in times of celebration.

Some attribute the breaking of the glass to the Talmud (TAHL-muhd = a book dedicated to the interpretations by the rabbis of the writings in the Torah), citing a story from a rabbi who, upon seeing a son's wedding celebration getting a bit too rowdy, broke a glass to calm down the revelling.

Bonus Tips:
- A glass lightbulb may be substituted, since it's thinner and more easily broken. Because it makes a louder and more distinct "pop," it will end the ceremony with a bang!
- Both the bride and the groom may break one glass together, or they can have two glasses — one for each of them to break.

Tip #16

Hip, hip, horah!
[HOR-ah = highly energetic celebratory circle dance, sometimes called the *chair dance*]

Yay, you're officially married! It's time to party!

And a great way to kick off the party is to invite your guests to the dance floor to participate in one of the most iconic features of the Jewish wedding celebration: the horah!

The *horah* is a traditional circle dance, typically danced to the music of the Israeli folk song *Hava Nagilah* (translated, that means "let us rejoice").

At the center of the dancing crowd, the bride and groom are hoisted into the air on chairs while friends and family dance in a circle around them.

Bonus Tip: Check ahead with the venue coordinator to see if they can provide an armchair rather than a side chair, so you've got something to hold on to as you bound around the room!

Tip #17

Yichud. . . or *yichud* not!

[yi-KHOOD = private time for the bride and groom immediately following the ceremony]

You've worked to plan the perfect wedding celebration. Entertained your guests. Signed your ketubah. Walked down the aisle. Joined your beloved under the chuppah, and recited your vows. Wow, you two could sure use a break from all the excitement! And if you're following the ancient tradition of *yichud*, then you're about to get some real personal one-to-one time with your sweetheart!

The term *yichud* refers to a tradition in which the newly married couple gets to break away from the wedding reception and meet each other in a private room so that the two can connect with each other in seclusion — and *yes*, they may even consummate their union before heading back to rejoin the party. It's not required to do so, of course, but no one will try to stop you if you do.

Now go make some babies, 'cause the in-laws want grandchildren. Pronto!

Tip #18

Chai! It's almost time to say good-bye.

[CHAI sounds like "Hi" = Hebrew word and symbol that means "life"]

In addition to the many Jewish wedding traditions, there are endless non-religious traditions that you may want to incorporate into your celebration.

Toss the bouquet? Sure, why not?! Feed your betrothed that first slice of wedding cake?
Of course. Bon appétit!

Feel like donning something old — and something new? Borrow something — or include something blue? Go for it! Wanna wave farewell to your guests dodging handfuls of tossed birdseed as you shuffle out to a getaway car dragging strings of tin cans behind? If that is your desire, do it. It's *your* day. Enjoy every part of it!

I'll close here at Tip #18, which, by the way, is a lucky number in Judaism, represented by the values of the Hebrew letters that form the word *chai*, which means "life."

I wish you "L'Chaim," a toast to the happy couple for a happy life together!

Mazel tov!

ABOUT THE AUTHOR

MARCELLE SIRKUS

[mar-SELL SIR-kiss = Your favorite Shiksa-Jew]

Marcelle Sirkus is a writer, living in Los Angeles with her teenage son.

Marcelle married her beloved, Frederick Brand, in April 2004. It was a gorgeous wedding with all the trappings of a modern yet traditional Jewish affair. There were guests a-plenty, lots of room to dance to a playlist of classic 70s disco and R&B, and oodles of schmoozing as top-shelf martinis flowed through a glorious ice-sculpture luge!

Their wedding and their marriage was filled with love, laughter, family, and Jewish traditions — some by the book, and others adapted to suit their personal values and preferences.

Marcelle lost her husband in 2016 after a sudden and unexpected illness. And though the pain of his loss hardly wanes over time, Freddy's memory remains a blessing to all who knew him.

To answer a question that many have asked following *A Shiksa's Guide to Shabbos: Don't blow out the candles!* — Marcelle wrote about an arrangement that she had with her son, that if she sold 1,000 copies of that book then she would get her son a dog.

Though the book sold very well, Marcelle wasn't convinced that getting a dog was the right move for them at the time.

They got a cat instead. Cleo's been a wonderful addition to their family.

Illustrations

Image credit "Wedding Couple" by Daniel Naranjo

Image credit "What is a Shiksa" by Daniel Naranjo

Image credit "Cupid's Bow" by Jemastock/Alamy Stock Vector

Image credit "Calendar" by Studio_G/Shutterstock.com

Image credit "Yiddish Scrabble" by vinnstock/Shutterstock.com

Image credit "Wedding Rings" by kelovskyco/Shutterstock.com

Image credit "Yarmulkes" by HardtIllustrations/Shutterstock.com

Image credit "Ketubah" by SigDesign/Shutterstock.com

Image credit "Milk" by Lineicons freebird/Shutterstock.com

Image credit "Meat" by Martial Red/Shutterstock.com

Image credit "Chuppah" by mimit2007/Shutterstock.com

Image credit "Mikvah" by NotionPic/Shutterstock.com

Image credit "Bedeken" by Lorelyn Medina/Shutterstock.com

Image credit "Hakafot" by Clipart.com

Image credit "Seven Blessings" by Clipart.com

Image credit "Tallit" by Clipart.com

Image credit "Kiddush" by infini/Shutterstock.com

Image credit "Break the Glass" by Olga Kuevda/Shutterstock.com

Image credit "Horah" by Clipart.com

Image credit "Yichud" by 3dfoto/Shutterstock.com

Image credit "Chai" by Zoart Studio/Shutterstock.com

Image credit "Author Portrait" by caturchandra

If you enjoyed *A Shiksa's Guide to Jewish Marriage*
you might like these other books, too!

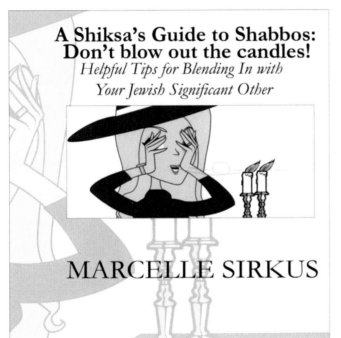

@shiksabooks   shiksabooks.com

Made in the USA
Middletown, DE
12 December 2022